DADDY'S CAP IS ON BACKWARDS

Bil Keane

FAWCETT GOLD MEDAL • NEW YORK

A Fawcett Gold Medal Book
Published by Ballantine Books
Copyright © 1996 by Bil Keane, Inc.

Distributed by King Features Syndicate, Inc.

All rights reserved under International and Pan-American Copyright Conventions. Published in the United States by Ballantine Books, a division of Random House, Inc., New York, and simultaneously in Canada by Random House of Canada Limited, Toronto.

http://www.randomhouse.com

Library of Congress Catalog Card Number: 95-96165

ISBN 0-449-14816-5

Manufactured in the United States of America

First Edition: June 1996

10 9 8 7 6 5 4 3 2 1

"I know what 'running to' is,
but what's 'fro'?"

"There's one good thing about
playin' basketball..."

"Mommy, would you spread
newspapers between here
and the bathroom?"

"Why do they call this my birthday suit? I wear it every day."

"Who dealt this mess?"

"I can't walk to Max's house.
He lives way over in a
different zip code."

"Who wrote '24 blackbirds' on
my grocery list?"

"This cat is makin' snake
noises at me."

"If we are what we eat, I don't
want to be a cauliflower."

"He wants you to taste his bottle Grandma. Just don't drink ALL of it."

"Her real name is Thel, but we call her Mommy for short."

"Mommy, how fast do
trees grow?"

"But, this IS a well-balanced meal. See?"

"Night-night! Don't
let the bedbugs
bite!"

"Who do you think is a better
actor — Bart Simpson or
Fred Flintstone?"

"That takes care of SECOND
grade. How many does that
leave for me to do?"

"One kid is being recycled
through second grade."

"Put your dirty clothes in
the hamster."

"To conserve water I volunteer to take less baths."

"Mmm! That's like sunshine in my nose."

"Can I answer when she says
'paper or plastic'?"

"Jason Fox draws funnier
cartoons than you. He can draw
spiders and slime and nooses
and ghouls and..."

"Dogs are the best pillows 'cause
they're always warm and soft."

"Is it okay to say 'Happy Father's Day' to Father Ben?"

"Horses are lucky. Their shoes
are nailed to their feet."

"The alphabet on pianos only
goes up to 'G,' then
starts over."

"Whenever we play store Dolly
gets to be the doot-doot lady!"

"Careful, Jeffy. This is a bad
place to drop your gum."

"Couldn't we take him to
the vet's?"

"Here it is — he's a
scarlet teenager."

"Who says mommies
can't jump?"

"Boy, it sure is human out today."

"God put the sky up out of reach
so little kids can't touch it."

"Come here a minute, Mommy.
PJ wants to show you
something."

"Dogs hate badminton 'cause
shuttlecocks don't roll."

"Could I have some trail mix,
Mommy? My team
is trailing."

"What happens if a bird is
afraid of heights?"

"Mommy, can we go back to the
Grand Canyon? My T-shirt
is gettin' tight."

"That water sure is fidgety."

"Your little brother looks a lot like
my little brother."

"All we've taken in so far are
I.O.U.'s from Daddy. His money's
in his other pants."

"Mommy, will you put more corn
beans on this bone?"

"I quit throwin' tantrums 'cause
they take so much
out of you."

"He followed us home. Can
we keep him?"

"I didn't know dominoes was a
game. I thought it was
just a pizza."

"Do butterflies have flower
petals for wings?"

"God answers ALL our prayers.
But sometimes the best
answer is 'no.'"

"It's a good thing I happened to be going through the trash!"

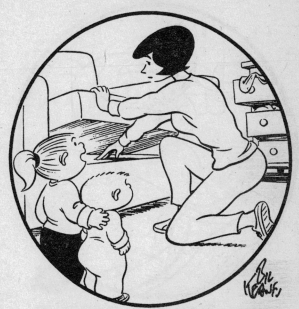

"Don't worry, Mommy. As soon
as PJ learns to talk he'll tell you
'zactly where he hid your keys."

"Mommy! The Tooth Fairy gave
me a cost-of-living raise!"

"Tell me a story, Mommy,
and put me in it."

"When my hands are in water a
long time they get wrinkled.
Why do fish stay smooth?"

"Down the wrong way? I thought there was only ONE way down."

"Jeffy's tryin' to feed pizza to
our turtle again!"

"Grandma's TV is really neat!
You hafta twist a knob to
change channels!"

"But, Billy! A SMALL allowance prepares you for a lifetime of small salaries and for your Social Security payments."

"Lunch is ready, and the venue
is the kitchen."

"Mommy, are these brown things
calories or just chocolate chips?"

"Did PJ get borned on the
right day or was he an
immature baby?"

"I finished first! Do I get
a gold medal?"

"When I punch in Grandma's number it sounds like 'Old MacDonald had a farm'..."

"Slow down, Mommy! PJ
can't keep up!"

"It can't be a fir tree, Dolly. The
bark's not soft enough."

"I know we're recycling now, but
can't you at least wait till
I'm finished?"

"Your feet get to ride in
those little swings."

"I wish we could turn down
the volume on thunder."

"Is this tomato ready
to be picked?"

"My grandma hasta have an operation 'cause she has a Cadillac in her eye."

"Next dance, can I
lead, Mommy?"

"Don't you know anything, Jeffy?
Phones don't have ZIP codes —
they have AERIAL codes."

"There's one more gulp left,
Mommy. We saved it
for you."

"Dolly hit my elbow with
her head!"

"I was just teachin' PJ to share."

"This delegation casts four votes
for pizza for dinner!"

"Does 'love thy neighbor' mean
the people on BOTH sides
of our house?"

"How do you know you don't
like it if you haven't
even tasted it?"

"I'm pretendin' the light goin' off
and on is lightning."

"Why do you keep letting your beard grow if you're just gonna shave it off anyway?"

"This is how I'm gonna be on
MY baseball card."

"Not so far out, Daddy."

"Shh! I'm listening to Ariel sing
'Part of Your World.'"

"I wish an aircraft carrier would
go by and make some
big ones."

"Hurry, Daddy! My bucket's
swimmin' away!"

"Maybe it's time for mothers
to unionize."

"We're helpin' you fill in the
empty spaces in the
dishwasher."

"You call THAT a burp?
Listen to THIS!..."

"I used to be a beautiful baby."
"But then you grew up."

"How can I put everything in its place when most of this stuff doesn't HAVE a place?"

"When Grandma was in school they didn't have computers and calculators. They used slates and chalk."

"Look at the neat bread Daddy
bought! It isn't even sliced!"

"You can tell the Pope is a good guy 'cause he always wears white."

"They'd have a LOT of different
Michael Jacksons to choose from
if they ever put him on a stamp."

"Our vacation pictures are still
in the camera."

"There are lakes, rivers and
streams, but I still like
puddles best."

"No thanks. I don't do
carrot sticks."

"Do we have some stiffer
kite string?"

"I wish they'd invent 'Monday
Night Cartoons.'"

"I'm glad Garfield doesn't live around here. He'd be a bad influence on Kittycat."

"Hi, Daddy! Did you know I
learned how to dial
the telephone?"

"Red!" "Purple." "Green!"

"If you have a scary dream
tonight, Mommy, I'll come
and get in bed with you."

"I put in too much bubble bath."

"Should I wear this shirt tucked
in or tucked out?"

"The reason we say grace is
to let dinner cool off."

"Grandma says the future isn't
what it used to be."

"Could I just stay up till the next commercial?"

"Gee, THAT wasn't long!"

"Billy lost another tooth, so he
limps when he talks."

"Can I change my name,
Mommy? 'Billy' has some
stupid rhymes."

"Those are the house's bones."

"...this little pig stayed home.
This little pig had
roast beast..."

"Know what kind of dog I like best? Cockle Spaniards."

"Billy called me a dweeb.
Is that a bad word?"

"Why do they always run into the pile?"

"There's no school today. Some weeks have bigger ends than others."

"I like Grandma's chairs. They
have place mats for
your head."

"MOMMY! HONEY'S HOME!"

"They don't look like hands
to me. They look
like ARROWS."

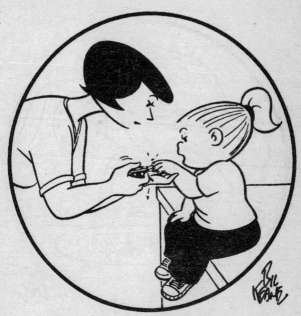

"If you cut my nails too short
I won't be able to
peel crayons."

"More smashed potatoes,
please."

"After 10 comes 19. Next is 11.
Very Good. Now to 16,
then 25, 20, 17..."

"Is dessert a la carte the kind
they wheel up to
your table?"

"Daddy, am I a Publigan or
a Demmycrap?"

"Is it okay if we draw goalposts
on the side of the house?"

"While you're lookin' at the report
card I'll be in my room practicin'
being grounded."

Keep in touch with the family.
Read more of the Family Circus®
by Bil Keane.